ANCHOR BOOKS

POETS TODAY

Edited by

Heather Killingray

First published in Great Britain in 1997 by
ANCHOR BOOKS
1-2 Wainman Road, Woodston,
Peterborough, PE2 7BU
Telephone (01733) 230761

HB ISBN 1 85930 499 0
SB ISBN 1 85930 494 X

FOREWORD

Anchor Books is a small press, established in 1992, with the aim of promoting readable poetry to as wide an audience as possible.

We hope to establish an outlet for writers of poetry who may have struggled to see their work in print.

The poems presented here have been selected from many entries. Editing proved to be a difficult task and as the Editor, the final selection was mine.

Poets Today captures all aspects of life ranging from 'new beginnings' to wildlife. It has been assembled from poets from all walks of life. Poets share with us their own unique style and flair for poetry. Each issue raised by the poet, gives us an insight on a subject they find close to their heart. All verses are varied in theme thus giving us a wonderful and delightful collection.

I trust this selection will delight and please the authors and all those who enjoy reading poetry.

Heather Killingray
Editor

CONTENTS

TOMORROW

Let's not reflect on things gone by.
The old year's gone, wipe that tear from your eye.
Look to the future, be hopeful, be bold.
All those adventures, yet to be told.
Whatever comes along, do your best,
Let's not others, tolerance test.

We're given choices, resolutions we make.
Don't be too far reaching, they're easy to break.
Let's not be selfish, angry or demand.
Let's try and be more kind, give others a hand.

Well things won't always be happy and fair,
Sadness and grief, we'll have our share.
But how we tackle what comes our way,
Is what will influence tomorrow's new day.

We're free to wonder, to come and go,
The choices are ours, yes or no.
The options endless, opportunities wide,
This way, that way any way we decide.

So let's make this our ultimate test,
To make this year, simply the best.
Don't put off till tomorrow what can be done this day.
Think what it is . . . you want your life to say!

Mabel Morris

THE LONGEST JOURNEY

My palms were sweating profusely
My heart was thudding too
I gulped for the hundredth time
What on earth could I do?

I couldn't eat my morning meal
My stomach felt so tight
I paced around and nearly cried
I'd been up most the night

A few hours to go, it isn't right
I look sadly at a knife
There is one way to avoid it
The longest journey of my life

I shall never see my friends again
All my girlfriends, far and near
My happy life, it will be over
Can I help but shed a tear?

I get into my prison clothes
At least I shall look smart
As I face the priest who condemns me
With a brave front, and a stout heart

He speaks softly to me, reassuring
I feel an angel by my side
Then the fears all disappear
As I turn to kiss my bride.

John Gorman

A NEW BEGINNING

A new year, a new beginning,
I feel joy and a start for singing,
For I can start afresh,
Something gained nothing less,
To be a better person,
More happy and fun,
Not to moan,
Or start to groan,
For this is a chance to start a better,
I shall contact my friends more and write them a letter,
To let them know of this better person I have become,
Will they recognise me and know who it's from,
I shall wake feeling cheerful,
And not at all dull,
Be more pleasant and understanding,
Rather than to just start ranting,
Stand up to people rather than just run,
I sound better already and I haven't even begun.

Louise Corke

CROSSING THE RUBICON

I turned over a new leaf today
And went into the spare room
To sort through all the bags of my past
And discard the things I no longer use.

I spent all day in the spare room
The clothes were all over the floor
And I took the time to remember
Where I was when I wore them before.

I spent all day in the spare room
I sneezed through the dust
And wandered down pathways
Of the memory of each item.

Has something so vital been missing
That I should cling on to my past
Leaving scant room for the present
And filling up spaces so fast.

Why do I need all this stuff?
There has to be a clue somewhere
Or perhaps the right outfit
Maybe then I could let the rest go.

Happy clothes, sad clothes, brave clothes
But no ordinary clothes to throw away
Beneath that new leaf was an old one
That I turned with such promise today.

Julia Wallis-Bradford

BLESSING IN DISGUISE?

There came a vandal, brick in hand
Who, for sheer 'devilment' one day,
A Christian bookshop window broke,
Then, cowardly, he ran away.

But to the pavement 'midst the glass
That shone in pieces on the ground
Fell prayer cards, hitherto unsought,
Which breezes scattered all around.

The devil rubb'd his hands with glee
When of the deed at first he heard;
Then angered that he'd 'double-crossed'
Himself and helped to spread the Word . . .

Susan Devlin

A NEW YEAR

A brand new year, what do I say
I'm going to start my diet today
With eating everything, all through the year
I can't fit in to any of my gear
Cakes and sweets, they are so tasty
They are also very weighty
I can't afford to put on any more weight
So I'm prepared to diet and wait
I'm not going to cheat, or pretend
Just see the results at the end
When I'm dieting, week after week
I can be slim, nice and sleek
I need to be weighed, so I can see
There's a club you can join, costs a small fee
So slimming world, here I come
To lose my thighs, hips and bum
Well here you go, I've lost two stones
Now I'm going to buy new clothes.

Maria Porter

A PERFECT WORLD

A unique place, existing only in dreams,
A place where every living being is loved,
Every life cherished and respected . . .

A place to be proud of and to respect,
Where the abandoned are cared for
The frightened are comforted and the rejected become loved.

A place where all life is equal.
With no leaders and no followers
Where prejudice is unknown and where spite is forgotten.

A place with no aggression or war
Where the homeless are housed
The hungry are fed and the ill and diseased are cured.

A place with no crime, no criminals and no punishment
Where families are friends
And friendships eternal.

A place with no cruelty and no suffering,
No pain or sadness.
Where hatred is unknown and fear is unheard of.

A place where death is a prize for living,
The unique ending to a unique beginning,
That is a perfect world.

Amy Lithgow

NEW YEAR - NEW LEAF?

All round the world, there are shouts of mirth -
As bells give welcome to the new year's birth,
Hands circled round - one great family
Wondering, 'What will the new year bring for me?'
One says 'Please hold out in store
Much better luck than I've had before -
I have had my share of the good things of life
But a little more would cause less strife.'

The rich man stands at his wide-open door
Surveying fields and land - and wishes for more
To grow bigger grain crops - to put in store
With never a thought for the hungry and poor
He then lies asleep, content in his bed
While the destitute watch for the day in dread!

O Lord, give us hearts that are thankful each day
Living the new year, as You show us the way
Bearing our loads with a cheerful smile
Happy to know You are there all the while
Giving thanks for a measure of strength and health
So much more precious than stores of wealth -

Then would the world be a happier place
For every colour, creed and race
Remembering that You are the life, truth and way
Our hearts content each and every day
Never craving for riches or wealth or money -
Your ways are sweeter, much sweeter than honey!

Rose Cooper

I WONDER

My new year resolutions made,
I'll write more poetry!
It's such a *good* part of the year,
Full of hopes and dreams.
And as we all plan far ahead,
What will the future be?

It is a time for having faith,
To be of strong resolve,
While giving welcome to the new,
And casting off the old.
A time for saying, *yes I will*!
A time for being bold.

I think of generations past;
The resolutions made;
And as they drift upon the years,
Were many made in vain?
Or did they ever change the world?
Perhaps we'll know one day.

Diana Gale

IT'S NOW OR NEVER

I look and see how fat I am,
I really must lose weight.
I sit and look at all that food,
Just lying on the plate.

It's now or never, I've got to start,
I'm afraid it's the middle-age spread.
If I don't lose it now I never will,
It's the thing most women dread.

It lays on your hips and stomach too,
And you try to hold everything in.
But at that crucial moment -
It all flops out and you wish you were thin.

You start some exercises and jogging too,
And hope it'll do the trick.
But shedding those pounds are agony,
And they're not shedding very quick.

Well it's got to be something drastic now,
You really just can't fight it.
You must admit, it's what you're dreading,
But you must go on that diet!

Linda Kersey

LATE DECEMBER BLUES

Snow-clad scene.
Blank, grey screen;
Domestic strife,
Stressed-out wife.

Pent-up boy
Short on joy;
Older daughter -
Happier, sorta.

Boxes of chocs.
Frozen locks;
Wintry walks,
Desultory talks.

The eagles wail,
As Christmas pales,
'Your lyin' eyes'.
A new year's nigh.

The future holds
Hope for the bold.
What's in store?
Don't know for sure.

That rock band
Always is at hand:
'Take it to the line
One more time'.

Wes Ashwell

ONE PIECE OF ENGLAND

The garden is our piece of green
To keep the grass neat and lean
But difficulties arise when weeds appear
Digging them out can cost you dear
Medicine for the ground is what they say
More money from your pocket to make pay
Climatic changes are causing the rot
When trying to keep flowers on your plot
Should one decide to change appearance
With weeds about, makes no difference
They grow in all weathers, no matter how you try
Although at times can make one tearful and cry
Hoeing, digging, mowing to remove
The weeds seem to make their own groove
Surely they will die and leave flowers to survive
Hoping at last to keep the garden alive
Leaves for compost to soak all around
But weeds reappear back in the ground
Perhaps we will win the battle at last
Next year possibly if we are fast.

Anthony Higgins

THE NEW ME

Who is this person I'm trying to hide?
Who I keep locked up and chained up inside?
Would I be a better person if she were set free?
Or would she take over the being of me?

Would people consider her better than I?
Would the person I used to be curl up and die?
Would the person she was be better in life?
Do you think she'd have made you a better wife?

Can I be that stronger, more dynamic girl?
And my life be wrapped in a social whirl?
Will I be the type to have men falling at my feet?
Or will I forever be stuck with this deadbeat?

Alison Harvey

LIFE

The leaves of life are as an open book
Admire the leaves, its daily content bear.
There's life in leaves whilst on a tree,
It's drawing from the root we see.
So tend the root and keep it good.

Who is the gardener?
Who tends our tree?
Who makes it good?
And who knows just what to do?

He is the unseen hand of God
He is the root - just look.
What are our branches drawing from?
The tree of life
And the leaves are for the healing of the nations.
Leaves have fallen - new leaves have come.
New leaves

A H Hoyle

IF I COULD BE A FLOWER

A garden full of flowers is wonderful to see,
If I could choose to be one which one would I be?

Hail the golden daffodil dazzling like the sun,
He trumpets loud and clear another spring has come.
What about the bluebell swaying to and fro,
Chiming to the honey bees come in, come in, don't go.

There's the lonely wallflower hoping that by chance,
The wind will come to visit her and make her petals dance.
I like the coloured pansies with faces Oh so gay,
Who cheer up love lies bleeding, who's extra sad today.

Would I choose the violet so small and very shy,
Trying to stay hidden from all who pass her by.
The violas sweetly playing in the setting sun,
The busy lizzies resting, their working day is done.

As twilight comes a-creeping the Chinese lanterns there,
To light the evening primrose whose fragrance fills the air.
If I could be a flower, an honour it would be,
They are, by far, in every way more beautiful than me!

Anne Berry

WORDS

When you want to say 'I love you' it's
Only words, when you want to say
'I need you' it's only words, and even
When you say 'I miss you' it's only words.
But words can say so much when you're
Sad and all alone, when the pressures
Of life you face, you're fighting on your own.
No-one knows just how you are feeling
Or the pain you're going through,
But with a warm, tender touch
From the one you love so much,
Can make a world of difference to you.
The burden is much easier to bear,
When you know someone truly cares,
Who's seen you through the good times and bad
Given you courage you never knew you had
Till you could make it on your own.
Everyone needs a shoulder to cry on,
That special person to help you see things through,
That's why my friend, my lover
I'll always be in love with you.

Shirley Seyfi

ANOTHER BROKEN RESOLUTION

No thanks, I'm on a diet and off all fatty
Food. I'm counting up the calories to keep
Me in the mood. I can't stand sweetener in
My tea, it really makes it bitter. Do you
Think with a month of this I will feel fitter?

Shopping is a nightmare. That smell of new
Baked bread! The sight of 'gooey' creamy
Cakes, I buy fresh fruit instead. I'm off
The creamy doughnuts, don't offer me chocolate
Cake. The larder is a danger zone and I
Daren't begin to bake.

I cook with vegetable oil and cut down on the
Bread but my tummy really rumbles as I lay
Upstairs in bed. I do so long for a midnight
Feast! Quick, try to get to sleep. I toss
And turn, no, it's no good, down the stairs
I creep.

I first look at the fruit bowl, I really
Don't fancy a pear. Oh dear! Why do I have
To be so fat? It really isn't fair.
This all takes so much self-control and that
I haven't got. So I took six chocolate snowballs
And ate the bloomin' lot!

Jean Watson

I'M SO IN LOVE

I'm so in love, it's hurting so much,
All I want, is you to touch.
I feel so alone when you're not here,
Have I lost you? Well that's my fear.

I'm so in love, it's tearing me apart,
I just want you, so we can start.
To get on with our lives and leave the past,
And be a couple, at long last.

I'm so in love, and miss you too,
When you were here, I wasn't blue,
But now you've gone, I'm totally lost,
So much so, I've paid the cost.

I'm so in love, you are my life,
And I pray to God, you'll be my wife,
So we can live, so happy as one,
And we'll realise what's done is done.

I'm so in love, that I'd rather die,
Than lose you to some other guy.
I want you more each passing day,
And I hate my life, since you went away.

I'm so in love, but so alone,
All because of the love you've shown,
I want and need you, here with me,
And I hope that one day, you'll agree?

Frank Sommerville

KEEPING A DIARY

To write in my new diary gives pleasure to me,
The events of the new year I cannot foresee.
I've kept full-length diaries since the age of fifteen,
A record of feelings and events they have been.

I confide in my diary as well as in my friends,
Expressing my views on the good and bad life sends.
I scribble in it hastily last thing at night,
It has no literary merits, but for me it's right.

A self-indulgent hobby, you're saying? Maybe.
It's very useful, I can check events you see.
I don't think they'll be studied for GCSE,
But never mind - to write in them is fun for me.

Heather Middleton

PEACE?

The new year preaches peace to one and all.
A worthy aim if understood by everyone
And reacted to, or else we all fall
Into disarray, all deals undone.
Too much to hope, it seems, for lasting peace.
In lands where terrorism is ever rife.
The faceless murderers will never cease
From mindless destruction and taking life.
If new year hopes were all lumped into one
With wishes, would resultant global mess
Be enough to halt the use of just one gun?
Never mind the armour held but to impress
The weak. Wouldn't it be stupendous
If worldwide prayer benefits all of us?

Richard Saunders

STARRY EYED

Fireworks explode
As the year begins,
Flashing like jewels
In the black iced skies.

Showing how bright
The future can be
If we open our hearts
As wide as our star-gazing eyes.

Mary Ellis

JANUARY SALES . . .

The shops are full of bargains galore,
They have more stock than they had before.
Where does it come from, no-one knows,
Bargains from our heads to our toes . . .

We push and pull and fight each other,
Everyone's gone mad and we head for cover,
I buy a hat, a glass, a dish,
Then realise, I don't need any of this . . .

My hair's a mess, I need more cash,
My train is due, it's time to dash,
I love the sales, I don't know why,
But I hope this year will hurry by . . .

L Lutfi

TRANSFORMATION

The old back yard was in an awful mess.
Old bicycles, rusty tins and mattresses.
In despair I went to bed cursing the world
For having the gall to fling its rubbish over my garden wall.

All was so still and silent when morning dawned,
And I leaned upon my window sill to behold a scene of pure delight.
For all had been transformed in one short night.
Snow had hidden all the ugly things, old bicycles, rusty tins and
mattresses
Were decked in robes of lacy white.

When spring comes and the shabby yard is seen again,
May the icicles in my cold heart melt, and show a life transformed.
To find the world a friendly place.

Gwendolen Bunch

BELIEVE

Two things I know
None can deny
All will err
All will die.

But one thing more
Do not grieve
All can learn
All achieve.

Tom Wood

GOOD INTENTIONS

Each year we intend to turn over a brand new leaf,
We start off with good intentions, soon a lot too brief,
As each brand new year comes swinging quickly around,
Those fresh well-meant resolutions, are speedily found.

All those old bad habits, we gleefully sweep right out the door,
We won't be moved, we will stick to our guns, of that we are sure,
But alas all those best laid plans of mice and men,
Seem to be flushed down that drain, it seems we have failed again.

We will grit our teeth, and try again this is no joke,
But alas our fag stopping habit, has just gone up in smoke,
Once more a great big effort, take a deep breath, turn another leaf,
And this time be certain our resolution, won't be so brief.

Let's try a strong-willed effort, to lose some unwanted weight,
Disaster struck the other night, when I got stuck in our front gate,
I guess we will just have to cut back on sticky cakes and currant buns,
Or I can see all those pounds and stones just turn into tons.

This is the year we are going to firmly make a pledge and swear,
That when we venture out again on our roads, we will take more care,
No more crazy fast speeds, ignoring one-way streets, in wrong gear,
And if we go down to the pub, we won't drive at all, if we had a beer.

I will definitely show more consideration and kindness, to fellow folk,
When they rile me up, instead of getting the needle, I'll try to see
the joke,
I guess we can all only keep trying, just attempt to lead a fruitful life,
Be it brothers, sisters, aunts, uncles, granddad, grandma, husband
or wife.

David Grant

SHADOWS

I cannot see light for shadows,
Shadows hanging over me.
I only see darkness,
Light I cannot see.

Everywhere I go,
Shadows are there.
Shadows of my past,
Blocking my path.

Shadows rise up from nowhere,
When things are looking good,
Confusing my direction,
Alone in the woods.

When I try to hide from the shadows,
They follow my every step,
Growing larger and larger,
Hanging over my head.

Gordon James Stowell

My Beautiful Lady

Gazing at the sky above
I see a face so full of love
That it can melt my heart of stone
And lead me to a greater throne

Beauty such I've never seen
For she must surely be a queen
I look at her with loving eyes
My lady up there in the skies

She looks at me with tenderness
This lady of such righteousness
For long ago, her son did die
For Judas he did tell a lie

Now as I gaze up at the sky
I see my lady give a sigh
She sees us all for what we are
My lady in the clouds so far

I feel I want to change my ways
For I saw the hurt there in her eyes
May her presence be with me all my days
My beautiful lady from the skies.

Mary Devine

THE BEAUTY OF THE LAND

Thank you God for our ears
To hear the birds sing high above
It shows their happiness and their love
For each day I hear them sing
I know it's another day nearer spring

The snow is falling all around
It's crisp, it's cold and falls with no sound
The sheep are lambing up on the moors
Hoping for sunshine and that it thaws

It's a miracle what we have on earth
The beauty of the land, flowers and birds
We are so thankful for this creation
From here in England and the rest of the nation.

Carol J Coles

FRONT PAGE

With babe in arm
And breast out bare
A gentle hand touched on soft skin

The face of beauty
Turned to its side
A sad, comforting expression, for her kin

The scene is set
Tainted like fading print
All this says front page 'Poetry Now'.

Michael Widdop

UNTITLED

A young lady with wonderful hair,
Has style unique and rare,
Her beautiful face,
Reflects God's grace.
She's the queen of all who care.

Anthony Davies

IT'S THE IRISH IN ME!

What do I see upon the telly?
One rather fat man around the belly.
Why is he so fat - my goodness
It's because he loves a pint of Guinness!

Now, though a large tum I have not got,
My love for a Guinness is on the dot,
For I've been told the dark brown drink,
Will keep you floating on air I think!

Howsoever that might be
I do still like a cup of tea,
But after a plate of fish and chips,
It's down my throat a Guinness slips ah!

Maisie Trussler

MANDY

I have a friend
I miss so dear
I haven't seen
For many a year
So please our Mandy
Before the baby's born
Reply to my plea
So I'm not so forlorn.

Anne Sunderland

THE PERFECT SNOB

Ecstasy sparking in the eyes
Of the perfect snob,
Facial movements condescending
                    Perhaps to sob,
Vivid lights of astounding
                    Self brilliance
Not so; my nobleless person, per chance.

Figure erect with self esteem
Even expecting to win the fight,
No-one is good enough nor so bright,
Sitting on a self made throne,
Doubly brazened when answering
                    The phone.

Littered with thoughts of infidel passion
Branded with self love
                    A perfect snob's fashion
Not a care in the world
                    For friends or foes
Illuminated with fireworks from head to toes.

The perfect snob has a
                    Gait so proud and selfish
Everyone else is an
                    Insignificant goldfish
Holding on one's own is physical strain
In spite of everyday agitation
Betrayed by others in the train.

Wake up to reality you perfect snob,
Take heed of others who might want to sob,
Be a devil and change your ways,
You'll never believe you have ever been,
                    So change, it pays.

Alma Montgomery Frank

A POEM FOR THE ANIMALS

The little calf new-born
He suckles from his mam
He seeks no more than comfort
Just like a new-born lamb
But what is this we see
They take him from his mum
They put him in a narrow crate
Doesn't matter he's only dumb
The lovely laying hen
They stuff her in a cage
She'll never nest or flap her wings
No wonder heaven's in a rage
The playful young spring lambs
The calves, the cows, the sheep
They're all transported miles and miles
It really makes you weep.

Bob Lewis

A SPECIAL FOSTER MOTHER

A mother's someone special
With a warm and gentle touch
A certain look that tells you
That she loves you very much

She's always very thoughtful
She's affectionate and kind
And she'll always listen patiently
When you've things on your mind

A mother's someone special
Who's a very lovely part
Of all the treasured memories
You hold within your heart.

E A Parkin

NOVEMBER

November is drab,
A cold, dark pit
A never-ending abyss
Of darkness and gloom.
The bright side of this month,
Is the exciting demons,
Demons of light and explosion
Fiery creatures dance in the night,
Then fall down a mere spark.
Exciting yet frightening the
Way they fly freely in the sky,
Almost like a bird.
The people are gone,
Excitement vanished.
The demons have been banished
For at least another year.
Everything is over,
No sun, no hope
No anything.
A thoughtless head
November is my least favourite month.

Lauren Sirey (10)

HEART & SOUL

I give you my heart,
I give you my soul,
I'd give you my world
If you never go.

I wanna hold you close under the rain
I wanna kiss your smile take away your pain.

I know what beauty is when I look at you
'Cause deep in my heart there's a picture of you.

You walked into my life to take my tears away
For as long as you're near I'll never feel lonely and cold.

My words of love that I speak to you,
Come from my heart and soul not from my voice.

I remember our first kiss
But it feels like you've forgot our last
All I see now is the painful past.

Pictures of our life she left behind
Memories of which she could not forget
And yet she can't see what love she still has.

Oh Lord how long can I go on being alone
Life will never be the same
Could this girl ever love me again?

Gary Miller

I MISS

I miss Regents Park
I miss our autumn walks
I miss Camden Market
I miss our Sunday expeditions
I miss Kiss FM
I miss waking next to you
I miss our daily chats
I miss dropping you off
I miss going to football with you
I miss our dodgy burgers
I miss Amsterdam
I miss writing your name in the snow
I miss the borderline
I miss our boozy heady nights
I miss helping you choose your outfit
I miss guessing your perfume
I miss meeting you in London
I miss following a couple arguing
I miss your kiss
I miss knocking on your door
I miss my heart beating faster
I miss Finsbury Park
I miss our madness adventures
I miss you being bolshie
I miss your laugh
I miss you being proud of me
I miss your smile
I miss how much you care
I miss holding hands
I miss falling in love
I miss . . . you

Alex Alexandrou

BROTHER POET

Good poems come from the heart of the man,
Brother poet is the one who really can.
Mixed words into sentences all do shine,
Brings joy to the reader the very first line.

He's got this talent and an excellent heart,
Let's take our hats off to his art.
Another poem accepted and he's at his height,
To add to people's hopes to bring such delight.

Positive poems he writes, it's a secret power,
Working with all those words into the evening hour.
Oh! Brother poet if the poems stop in future years,
Such deep misery will bring all those tears.

Philip Anthony Corrigan

PERSPECTIVE

Fifties adolescents
Staked out freedom
Inspired by rock'n'roll beat

Strident sounds
Of city life
It's melody
Rhythm enriched
Experience
Fed fantasies
Relationships
Enhanced sense
Of love despair . . .

Mature they evolve
Find city sounds discordant
Forcing dissonance
On residents who walk its streets
Trapped by jobs to city lives -
Measure freedom
By when and how
They can escape
Cacophony

Sound a retreat
To country lanes
Bird song Angelus . . .

Bettina Jones

HIAWATHA'S SIGNALMASTERING
(with apologies to that Long chap)

Through the darkness work the signals
Of the 30 Corps Headquarters.
Through the night they toil and struggle
Keeping up communications.
Routers routing in their foxholes
Queries calling to their partners
While the teleprinters - clicking -
Clear the lines behind the lines.

And the figures of the day's work
Are compiled by weary Supts.
While the Signalmaster dozes,
Dozes off in fitful slumber.
Tired of reading 'Five Red Herrings'
Tired of writing many letters
Tired of sitting, smoking, moping
Waiting for the morning's light.

Till the hour of brooms and dusters
Till the place is swept and tidied
Till the daily morning lines - state
Comes and goes with 'urgent' haste.
And the fresh and sprightly day shift
Drifting in on wings of song
Sends the gaunt and weary night shift
Crawling home to well earned rest.

M Scott-Morton

ROLL UP FOR THE SOUTH ASIAN TOUR

'Roll up, roll up for the South Asian tour,' cried the guide in his sleek
                                        grey helmet and body suit
We were straddling the Indian Ocean in Malé for sure.
'Welcome to the Maldives in Visit Maldives Year 3000',
Read the neon sign against a steel coconut tree.
The educated tourists landed in their shuttles - only an hour's flying
                                        time from London.
We were in a futuristic underwater paradise a complete beach resort,
                                        swaying coconut trees,
Glistening white sand, thatched huts beneath a huge glass dome.
Outside the turtles, multi-coloured fish and sea horses roam
Shoals of delight, a fusion of colour amidst the coral fields.
We saw in the distance the lights of adjoining domes -
More underwater resorts, bars, restaurants and shopping malls.
The shuttles whizzed the tourists - *dome hopping* - they called it
Between the Maldivian resorts - all indulging in the art of doing
                                        everything underwater.
To think a few centuries ago it took eleven hours to fly to the
                                        Maldives.
There were one thousand islands then - before the ocean swallowed
                                        hundreds, out of sight.
In the distance of time the Dhonis and the speedboats were the
                                        predecessors of the shuttles,
A quaint Maldivian Air Taxi and Hummingbird helicopter took
                                        them island hopping around the Dhivehi Raaje -
Now they fly in seconds in those magical spacecraft through the
                                        speed of light.

We moved to Sri Lanka, the paradise isle to the east of the Maldives.
The ancient monuments and rock carvings protected by transparent
                                        Domes.

The Milky Way rock group were synthesising away at the nightclub.
Sri Lanka's golden beaches were the cruel victims of the
                                        encroaching sea -
In place of beaches were space pads with nightclubs, floating
                                        restaurants in chrome,
The space age city of Colombo - neon signs lit the Asian sky,
The Sri Lankan cricketers were playing the Australians in the
                                        Kandy Astrodome.
We watched the match on the gigantic television screen
Erected for the inter-planetary cricket fans, on what was once Galle
                                        Face Green.
Then we boarded Air Lanka's space flight to the moon - a straight
                                        path from Adam's Peak.
Arthur C Clarke's premonition was now a reality, South Asia was,
                                        in all its density,
Tourism's space age frontier - for the educated traveller, the
                                        adventurous and the chic.

Ivan Corea

DISCREPANCIES

Nine fifty-eight it always was
With network card from here
To London with a third-off fare,
The first train you could use.
But now the management's decree
Forbids us by this train to go
Tho' suburb station of the town
Will let you in, two minutes on.

By bus to Tonbridge, then, I went
To catch that train at ten past ten.
At five to hour on platform there
'Where go you Miss? This train here
To London is - hop on fast!'
'Network?' No matter get on board
Ticket collector clipped my card
And London reached ahead of time!

K Stephenson

AUTUMN LOVE

I read of them daily, photos brand my mind. Abused, beaten,
some haven't eaten, starved of love unkind
world, random luck who rears, clips or kisses your ears.
Anne Frank, a saint succoured by time, dead before prime, or
maybe a child of foreign nation, bone thin in desolation.
How I prayed for the children beaten or who hadn't eaten,
and those whose parents were cruel . . . was I such a fool?
For having loved you, paving your path of protection,
striving for maternal perfection. Grieving for those
close at hand, third citizens left to roam, no-one at home
to cook their dinners, or kiss their scars.
Dying, so long I was dying, you never knew, I was your
carer so you could rest, I wanted you to have the best.
Was it a test and I failed?
For my cup spilled over with love. No callous clouts
nor shouts; never hit, had every kit for play.
And joined the Disney fun, whilst I lay dying in the shadows
of the sun. Why did you leave, what had I done,
didn't you love me, your mum?

Elaine Pomm

ONE OF A FEW (ONLY A FEW) VACANT HOLES

Spiders crawl low
in a catless house,
Everything stirs
especially the mice.

Gavin Clark

CROSSING THE THRESHOLD
(THE MYSTERIES AT ALDERGROVE AIRPORT)

'You are approaching the end
Of the moving
Walkway.

Please,

Be ready
To push your
Trolley over the ramp.'

Jens-Peter Linde

FROM A LAMENT; MOTHER FAITH

When lying on your dying bed
You smiled 'You must have faith' you said
Yes, dear mother, here's my faith, I know it will come to be
That those who labour, will create, classless society
Though men are holding back the birth, with utmost violence
With weapons which destroy the earth, for power, for pounds, for pence

Faith
Capital's power is shattered, money has lost the crown
Deep cracks are in its edifice, its walls are tumbling down
Nothing is permanent, fixed or set, all will be replaced
By a new form, within the old one, now encased
Now the time is being born when class and race will cease
Divisions between us all will everywhere decrease
And rich and poor will disappear and we will live in peace
The womb is ripe and ready now, the labour of birth has begun
For us to live as we should live and value everyone
And love and care for all living beings who flourish beneath
$\qquad$ The sun.

J M

THE COMPETITION

What shall I write? What shall I write?
I somehow can't think what to say
There's little time left for my entry in
As it's near to the closing day

I must quickly decide on some subject
What on earth can I write about
I've scratched my old head a hundred times
Yet nothing so far has come out.

Desperation drives me to take measures
As my head's in a spin I'll resort to a pin
I'll pick a page in my dictionary
And then stab the blessed pin in

It appears to be not very helpful
As it's stuck in the silly word 'Jam'
Could be plum, could be apple, or traffic
Though whichever I don't care a damn.

To help my old brain let's try the pin once again
This time the outcome might be clearer
Oh no! The word it gives me is 'Diarrhoea' I see
So a solution is getting no nearer

I don't think I'll use that pin anymore
To ignore it again does seem wrong
I'll therefore leave these lines as they are
And just send you the stanzas along.

J W Cash

GHOST TRAIN

There used to be a railway here,
Single track, of course.
No whistle can you hear
To signal the little tanker's coming;
Only the birds' high cry
And the bees humming,
Or a lowing cow
Break the silence now.

But in the night they swear,
Down at the farm,
Near the old tunnel's mouth,
(And contradict who dare!)
They hear her warning shrill
Echoing from arch to arch,
And hill to hill.
Maybe it's fancy; I don't know.
They scrapped her many a year ago.

Lionel F Gillam

MY LUMBERJACK SHIRT

My lumberjack shirt is nothing special
Just a friendly piece of clothing
Worn patches, odd buttons
All you could ask for
Comfortable and a favourite
And when I wear it
The most unremarkable thing you ever did see.

When she wears my lumberjack shirt
The Earth stops spinning
Time grinds to a halt
The shirt supports her radiance
Caresses her supple beauty
Shines in the shadow she casts
This is my lumberjack shirt
The most remarkable thing you ever did see.

Marcus Foreman

THE FIGHT

I know, believe me, what your hearing
Yeah, it sure sounds peaceful
And if I were you,
I'd listen in awe.
I guess you think

It's your pension
For you definitely deserve it.
Listen
To deaths sweet whisper.
Grasp it, chase it,
Follow it down yonder.
Drifting contentedly?
Tighten your grip

Around your very own neck
Pull the rope tighter
If you dare
Ha, after all, it's only a game.

But it's not over yet.

Christina E Ellis

THE KINGFISHER 7.10.76

Thou bird of the river, stream, beauty and song so sweet,
O dear kingfisher, how my very being welcomes thee here,
In England, Wales, and Ireland vast, - O great bird of cheer!
Thou doest hover o'er water-face, to catch fish with a gentle beat
From thy gay, short, rounded wings, which shall e'er greet
No man, but dwell with a sincerity in thy kingdom, while
thou doest appear,
Like some blue streak, flying, the heights so clear!
With thy mate, thou doest incubate thy eggs, beneath thy feet,
In a nest-hole in a quiet bank, o'er waters of a rippling stream;
O kingfisher, thou art alert with thy sharp chee- call,
It is so audible as thou doest fly above; O bird of my glory,
fill thou my dream,
With a never-dying enthusiasm, for thy world so primitive
and small;
In my heart's inner depths, there a quenchless human scheme,
Which longs to establish comprehension, of man and bird; what
in life's end for thee, - will
- befall?

Grace Devina Priest

GEORGE

What do you think sat there so mute
We think you're nice, ever so cute
Always a laugh, always a smile
But maybe if we sat awhile
And really thought to ourselves why?
Who has the power to sell and buy
Man's voice, man's arms, man's legs,
man's life,
Who has the power to take his wife
Away, just when he needs her most,
When he has nought else of to boast
This punishment, what is it for?
Was he so sinful long before?
They say he'll suffer till he learns
And then his right to die he'll earn.

Clare Moore

LOURDES VISIT

There was a child named Bernadette
She experienced something wonderful by a stream,
I too have visited this place and marvelled at what I've seen
It's where you find Christ's love flowing
And the love of Christianity forever growing
You'll find helpers and children
Both young and old
Loving caring sharing
It's a miracle to behold
Christ thank you for letting me visit,
I can now go and tell
Please listen this world
Our Lord is alive and well.

John Lavery

CHRISTMAS

Long time ago the angels said,
Peace on earth, and do not dread.
Let your lives be free from fear
The Saviour of mankind is here.

Some gave Him welcome at His birth,
Others thought He had no place on earth
They sought to kill, and Him destroy
While many hearts were filled with joy.

Joy that a Saviour had been born
Into a world which strife had torn.
Peace, Christ brought, to reign as king
Alas, His message was a rejected thing.

Today we still have a world torn apart,
For Christ has no place in many a heart.
Christians without Him cannot be
For peace, joy, goodwill, in Him we see.

God's plan for the world was all prepared,
That our life with others should be shared.
With loving care, not malice and hate,
Then Christians will the world translate.

Christmas begins in you and me
With this I'm sure we must agree,
It's not just the garlands and the tree
But thanks for our Lord's nativity.

John Waddington

TODAY SPEAK

That's £1.95, there you go, thanks a lot;
See you later.
Actually I don't know.
Surf the internet
tell me about it
Download, e-mail, fax
no problem; no sweat.

What's it about?
Don't even think about it!
Right, well . . .
actually you need to give me a bell.
No mobile, sorry about that
Is there a problem?
Not if you're a fat cat.
On a downer?
Get real!
Can I get back to you, we need to talk . . .
it's the feel-good factor, so feel!

It's ace
so interface.
PC on the blink?
You're grounded,
This needs a rethink, not.
Environmental awareness,
it's our global heritage, in all fairness.
The national lottery,
maybe I'll get lucky
You've got no chance
so back to the day job and those figures enhance.
Security alert in town
It's only today-speak, no need to frown.

M L Rose

UNTITLED

You can depend on your 'Elijah'
As long as God give him to you,
But remember that the time will come
When you will have to go on through.

No longer can he be your guide
God does not want him to stay
As you come alone to your Jordan
Like 'Elisha' you are filled with dismay.

Reluctantly you now reach Jericho
You faith in God is tested here
But it's where you will receive a sign
God is with you never fear.

Don't give up when you reach Bethel
Or panic though at wits end
God in His wisdom reminds you again
'No more 'Elijah' on whom to depend'

Put into practice what you have learned
Praise God for his mercy and grace
Praise Him for lending you His 'Elijah'
In glory you'll meet face to face.

Alice Carlin

HALLOWE'EN

Hallowe'en is in October
Trick or Treat is the youngsters' game
Coloured masks and knocks on the door
Heralds the start of this old strain
Old people wonder at this sight
Are they friendly, or will they fight!

Marie Barker

THE NIGHT SHIFT OF DREAMS

The night came down, gently, and with friendship, like a comfortable and cosseting blanket

It eased away all of the days pains, anxieties and disappointments. It washed, cared and caressed with the soothing anodyne of sleep.

During this restful period the mind was not hindered by the workaday tasks of existence

The mind could keep the restless brain engaged, sometimes with pleasant, sometimes unpleasant but always harmless, picture shows.

In this peaceful idyll of tranquillity, the thoughts of the day, could be sifted like fine sand, to find, perchance, a gem, an idea of irradiant clarity

This gem of thought, it might polish and burnish with fervour, rounding it off and making it free of the constraints of daily life.

At this time, there was availability of self questioning, there was the chance to disregard the fripperies of inconsequential distractions.

The day's energies could be absorbed, sifted, collated, catalogued and filed in the relevant cerebral reference library.

Alex Brown

EDITORIAL POLICY

'Nothing goes in that might offend -'
So ditch that 'ode to a skylark', my friend;
As a fly, I'm skylark food, you see -
Print 'ode to a skylark' and you'll offend me!

No poems in praise of beautiful roses -
Offensive to blind folk who've non-working noses.
No poems describing the garden mole,
Offending the people with lawns full of holes.

Not a word about having to work for your pay,
Upsetting job seekers searching 'sits vac' each day.
Nowt about education, that's contentious enough:
Is it teachers, or pupils, or the system that's duff?

No rhymes about dying or rhymes about living
(The newly bereaved can be most unforgiving).
'Nothing goes in that might offend -'
Ensuring that's true could drive Tim round the bend!

Sallie Copeland

FOG

So thick the fog all around.
Icy, cold and damp
Black clouds rest on the earth.
Black ice on the ground
Listen to the fog horn sound
Way out on the sea.
Warning, steering ship off the rocks.
A mournful sound it can be.
We walk slowly through the mist.
Not a soul in sight.
Only the cloud resting on the earth,
Eerie, and black as night.

Doreen Pertherick Cox

EASTER

It did not seem right that Jesus should die,
In oh such pain, because of me.
But where would I be without that cross,
He died in my place at such a cost.

Why Jesus should have such a fate,
He healed the sick, gave the blind their sight
He loved the people he came to save.
He loved, he died on Calvary's tree.

On Easter morn God raised him up,
And now he reigns with the Father above.
He rose that we might be with him
He freed us all from our sins.

Praise God for his only Son,
Who my salvation, my soul has won.
Thank God for His love for me.
And never let me forget Calvary.

Doreen Lough

THE OFFER YOU CAN REFUSE

Go on, take one.
No.
But you must!
Why?
Everyone does.
I don't.
Is there something wrong with you?
No.
But it's a party!
So?
You want to have a good time?
Oh yes!
Well take one then.
No.
You're scared!
No - but you are.
Me?
Yes - too scared to say no.

Viv Potts

A CUP OF TEA

A cup of tea,
For me would be.
An unfashionable cup of Ty-Phoo.
Brewed with boiling hot water,
And then left to stand.
For just a minute or two.

I once tried Earl Gray,
But was unimpressed.
And the Camomile was almost insipid.
While the lemon and ginger,
And the Moroccan mint.
Left a taste in my mouth that was wicked.

The nettle I tried in curiosity.
Likewise the peppermint and the wild cherry.
I've yet to try Chinese green tea.
Though I am told that it's drank by many.

Yes if I had the choice.
I would pick Ty-Phoo.
Brewed in the traditional manner.
I'd take it straight,
Without sugar or milk,
Then sip it at my own leisure.

T S Harris

VALENTINE

Vainly I tried to find the words
All the things I've seen and heard
Listened to waters and the breeze
Enchanting music in many different keys
Nothing seems fit to form a phrase
To make a sentence your fitness to praise
In spite of trying many ways
Nothing can I say or do
Except to whisper I love you.

Peter McCreary

OUR MAM

We were so proud of our dear mother
And thank the Lord we had no other
Four children we were, but one was so special
She worked so hard for us all, she had no time for pleasure.
Mum had a child with special needs, there was no time for leisure,
He was so ill, he could not talk, and would always be her baby.
Her tender loving care, was so special, mum was a dear lovely lady.
Mum kept him safe, always held his hand, but never said 'why me'
She worked so hard, always like a busy little bee.
In those days long ago, no help was given for a child like he
Mum only ever said 'what will be, will be'
She never had time for idle gossip, mum said a wise head, held a
still tongue
And never gossip about people you live among
Mum lived a day at a time, shedding many silent tears
No-one asked if she had hopes and dreams, but mum must have
had silent fears.
He has suffered enough, the Lord said one day, and gently led him
away.
Fifteen years she loved and cared for that special son.
But never once did her faith sway.
She cried until she had no more tears.
For a beautiful son, always in her heart she kept so near.
When mum went to heaven, Dennis was waiting with open arms
For our mum, whose love we all held so dear.
No presents can we give our special mum, but we all shed many a
silent tear.

Sylvia Roberts

FACE AT THE WINDOW

I gaze out of my window,
I look out at the world,
Some things are big, some are small,
Little children wave,
On their way to school,
Shouting, and laughing,
Playing the fool.

Still, I stand and wait a while,
For a wave from you.
And see you smile.
I laughed with you, I played your games,
The bond between us,
Is in our name.

What has happened, you must say,
Why can't I come again to play,
Was it something I said?
What have they done?
It was all for nothing,
My little one.

Soon one day,
You will stand tall,
We will sit and talk,
I will tell you all.

Patricia Cairns

HEIDI

I love my dog
she was a healthy
cuddly friendly dog,
she was 8 years old
she was a good
fun dog. We used to
take her out to the
woods and let her
off the lead. I love
her more than anything
in the world. She passed
away 3 years ago. Heidi
died of a bad heart, but
I have a photo of her in my room.

Lorraine Jacobs (11)

DECEASED

Grandad,
he died when I was small,
He made up strange stories to tell me.
He once told me, of all the foreign places he had been to,
hot, like Egypt,
places like Africa.
He's read stories to me.
I still think,
he let me beat him,
when we played tic-tac-toe.
I couldn't go to his funeral,
I was too young,
I still miss him.
His old,
wrinkly face,
with black moustache
and a bit of wispy grey hair, behind each ear.
His black framed glasses,
resting on his nose.
Now the book is closed forever.
He'll never be forgotten,
but he'll always be missed.

Laura Gillard (10)

To Begin With

There are roads without a sign
An unturned rock or two
I'm going to take those risks of mine
and to myself be true
I stumbled on my desire, my will
that I found deep in my heart
So now I will fight on until
no need for a fresh start
been clinging on to yesteryears
feel safe with the things we know
now it's time to face my fears
Chase a dream, let go.

Alison Cox

S O S

Hanging on to an imprisoned feeling.
Killing you off from outside to in.
Giving you a boost of once lost confidence
Helping you within the forever ending struggle
Embracing you with fear.
Moving only with breath of wind
Your mind pouring out its anxieties
Giving you just elements to think of
Water of life, Fire of hell
Earth of hope, light of rebirth.
The hours go by as the pendulum swings
The days reverse to reveal new pastures.
This eclipse puzzles your empty being
Which only forces your desires to burn.
Hate gives you nothing to grab hold of.
On the edge of love you balance feelings
Self respect eaten by your own fear.
Consciousness is lost for never knowing any better.
Given no other choice but the burning life below you
Beginning to drop in this pit of hell,
But as quick as you fall you rise,
Pulled up on the edge of darkness
Once again solid ground under your feet.
The surroundings of being free to live
All guilt dissolves
Free at last.

Marie Newman

DESERTED

There's a space that's on my towel-rack,
Where your bath-towel used to be.
And on the sill an empty glass
Once shared by you and me.

It once held both our toothbrushes,
Now the glass just holds my own.
It continually reminds me,
That there's just me all alone.

In the wardrobe are some dresses
The ones I liked to see you wear,
And in the drawer some undies.
I wonder why you've left them there.

I keep wondering why you've left me.
Is there some other man?
Please let me know, and quickly,
For I've taken all I can.

Gordon Barnett

THE DREAMER'S LIFE SENTENCE

My skin fits today,
When my heart's in my throat,
My head's in the clouds
And my thoughts are afloat
On a mirror-still river,
A sleepy soul sighs,
Reflects all the need
In the night of my eyes,
And the thoughts uplift me
Suspend me mid-air,
With the help of a moon,
And a star, and a prayer,
And a sunny horizon,
Keep nightmares away,
For believe it just might be
A very nice day.

Julie Ann Bell

NEW YEAR'S PROMISE

New Year's eve
I know there is my tomorrow
From thence a brand new year.
I have my hopes
I have my dreams
A family so precious so dear.
I want happiness for others
Their trials in life to be light.
Then me to make a New Year resolution
. . . This is only right.
I would like to save money
So in safety for things taken for granted
I can pay my way
I do smoke I would like to reduce it.
I enjoy to sit and write.
This a cup of tea.
Has given me many hours
Of pleasurable feelings
So to pack smoking up completely
Won't be a New Year's resolution for me.
I know next year to live my life
I am in God's hands.
I hope he gives me direction of purpose
My New Year's resolution will be
More his words to understand.

Victoria Joan Theedam

A NEW START

My resolution - to do something
new, something I have never
done before,

I should learn to drive a car
(but I bet I wouldn't get far)

I could take a trip abroad
(but I think I should be bored)

I might try a language course
(but that would leave me hoarse)

I should take in a lodger
(or would that be too much bother?)

I could train to sing
(but it's such a hard thing)

I might learn to ski
(but would that really suit me?)

Or perhaps I'll write a poem?

T Priest

NEW BOTTLE

If New Year was June
First, I could easily
Resolve to stop drinking so
Much and eating chocolate.
It would be a doddle to
Be civil to my neighbours,
And pat the dog.
How could I fail to be
Virtuous when the
Sun burns my whisky
Free brow, and the breeze
Plays over my no-fat
biscuits.
But no it's January,
Most god-awful month in
The calendar, lashing rain
And darkness pretending to
Be daylight, what could be
worse, February could be
worse, pass the bottle
Please.

Anthony Parkinson

A SONG FOR SUSAN

You, you mean so much to me,
And I find it hard to say,
These feelings spinning around my heart,
Each and every day.
The way you love me,
I just don't understand,
All comprehension leaves me,
When you take my hand.
The sensations I feel,
When you lay your hand upon me,
And touch me so softly;
I just don't understand why I feel the way I do
When;
When you're touching me,
And the way I feel for you
I find so difficult to explain,
For I've never felt this love before,
A love so strong it gives me pain,
Oh the love that comes from you Susan.

Kenneth Thornton

RESOLUTIONS FOR NINETY-SEVEN

People will hope in ninety-seven
  that their new made resolutions,
Will beat the hazards of today
  and find the right solutions.

They pray for peace upon the roads
  and that road rage disappears,
And that driving will be disciplined
  where one can drive without this fear.

Then their thoughts turn to those stalkers
  who are puzzling and complex.
They hope this trend is overcome
  with their threat to the fairer sex.

Then they wonder about those bullies
  in the army and our schools,
Will the authorities win the battle
  or will those thugs still rule.

Will our young men who are taking drugs
  turn over a new leaf,
To give their parents satisfaction
  instead of all the grief.

Those are some of the New Year resolutions
  people would like to see applied
As they are rife in our society
  that something must be tried.

Lachlan Taylor

MOTHER, IN OLD AGE

Resting, she lives her girlhood days anew -
Those joys and sorrows fresher with the years.
Her children once again play at her knee
Or held there, sleeping, lulled by her song
                                    - now too
His voice, who shared her life in love, - she hears
And all those happy hours again can see
With eyes un-dimmed. Still
her slight form resists.
Times ravages, she moves on youthful tread
While busy hands weave comforts tirelessly.
The innocence of wondering gaze persists
Transcending age. Time crowns her silvered head
Unbowed, she bears life's pain with dignity.
Our gentle mother gives us tender joy,
Such love, nor age nor death can yet destroy.

Clare Girling

TAKE A LEAP - IN THE RIGHT DIRECTION

A new year to start the things
    you really want to do
A pen, a sheet of paper, a jingle
    or two.
Words form the heart, rhyme from
    the soul.
Another year, a new start, that
    will fill the small hole.
Feelings inside, never put them
    to chance
It's like trying to learn the
    routine of a dance
So take that step before it's
    too late
Don't leave it too long, or
    tempt fate.

Kris Walke

NEW LEAVES

Another year has passed us by,
Let's have some peace from war and fight,
Let us all live as one,
Let the children have some fun

Let the sky be blue and bright
Let the sun cast a light
Let the trees be full of leaves
Flowers growing from tiny seeds.

Smiles on everybody's face
Little animals wild and tame,
Let's hope next year will be the best one yet
And thank the Lord for all we get.

Turn every corner
Turn ever light
Night and day let us see
If we can turn over a new leaf.

Deane Rhian

A NEW START

Our worries have piled up into a heap
Through the years
We have cried until we can take no more
Each worry is like another piece of old paper
Gathering dust in the cupboards of our minds
But the time has come to light the bonfire and
turn out our thoughts and fears.
Drop our worries into the bin ready for the fire
Tear up our fears, throw all the rubbish on
And watch it all burn to past's ashes
Gone forever.

Pauline Edwards

NEW LEAVES

New year resolutions what do they mean to me, I really cannot answer
They're never kept you see. New leaves well they're not really new
For every year's the same, you know you'll do the best you can. But
people still complain,
Some say you owe them money, but you paid them back last year.
But the publican at the King's Head says you owe him for the beer
When you held a party in February last year.
  New Year resolutions they really are a joke
    I can't give you an answer, you see I'm stony broke.
      Mary had a little lamb.
Mary had a little lamb she also had some prunes, a plate of tarts
Some chocolate hearts, and a tin of macaroons, a piece of skate
A piece of place and a portion of cod roe.
And when they carried Mary out her face was white as snow.

Alfred Cook

LOOKING FORWARD

Tomorrow's unknown moments wait
to greet us with surprise
when well-laid schemes and hopes and dreams
are dashed before our eyes.

When planning for the future seems
a foolish thing to do
to help us cope, we live in hope
that dreams sometimes come true.

As days may come and days may go
only time alone can say
if we can find some peace of mind
in all we do today.

J W Griffiths

POET'S DILEMMA

What is a poet I sometimes ask?
Seeking for treasure in words that last.

Do I pen the words of an age gone by?
It sounds so poetic to use, thee and thy.

I write of life, love and death,
These are the poems the public like best.

It's not the words we squeeze and tease
Or the lofty thoughts that rustle in
The breeze.

The melody of words is unique
But is this play on words all we seek?

The ancient Greeks wrote words so
Wise and divine,
So is the secret of writing from the
Heart or from the mind?

One more dilemma as we take up the pen.
Are we more bias to woman or
Bias to men?

Thomas Sutton

HYPED DOWN NEW YEAR

Here we go again,
all on a high,
it's going to be
different this year,
this time we're
really going to try.
We're going to be nicer,
thinner,
achieve our dreams,
do all, for the good
of the world,
get educated,
be dedicated,
stop, I'm exhausted,
just reading these themes.
So there's something new
I've decided to try,
just relax and enjoy
whatever comes,
ah, living at last.

But knows who what,
next year.

Daphne Smith

MY BROKEN RESOLUTION

I've made a New Year resolution
'Tis one I've made before
A not so simple resolution
To stop swearing, once and for all!

I've tried so hard not to break it,
So many times before.
Now here I am resolving it
For the umpteenth time or more.

I never sound off at the deep end
I'm far too refined for that,
I just use a swear word to emphasise
When the vicar, or friends stop to chat.

But occurrences will happen,
Just when I least expect.
That's the time when I do go blank,
And forget the proper text.

But this time I aim to conquer,
And strike it off the sheet.
I'm sure the vicar will be pleased
The very next time we meet.

Charles W Bayton

ORDEAL

Winter creaks and tears with
its icy grip
Around the staunch nobility of
a silent tree
Constricting and willing the
roots to rip
Yet the tree stands firm in
a merciless sea

Frost shelters and finds insidious
hold
In the weary branches and
gnarled trunk
Multiplying in the horrendous cold
To render the tree sapped,
bowed and sunk

A wind blows gustily from the
arctic north
Snapping the branches of the
lonely birch
He must endure - no warming hearth
As his weight is blown into
rock and lurch

Now the earth is tender, moist
and rich
The sun is shining and the
tree stands proud
Spring has banished the
wintry witch
As green shoots sprout
and rejoice aloud.

J A Shaw

FIRM RESOLUTIONS

New leaves on January 1st,
Is that realistic?
Just turn over a new leaf and carry on,
Instant recreation?
Or is it more involved than that
And needs more time, more work, more thought?

For new leaves - old ones have to shrivel and die.
A time of dormancy ensues
Like mourning for what's just passed,
Until new life flows through that withered frame
And buds appear
Which gradually mature,
And then, and only then
We get
New leaves.

Bob Hookins

A New Year's Warning?

Each new year begins with promises, resolutions,
- Perhaps to visit more our ageing relations.
Children promise to be good for mum and dad,
Chocolates and sweets are not to be had.
Mums promise to stick to a new diet,
We'll grill our food, not fry it.
Most promises will soon be broken
- They're just a new year holiday token.

But what if the whole of mankind
Were to make and keep a resolution so fine
- A promise that we will try to atone
To this world, for all the damage we've done.
- Disease, war, greed, pollution,
Oppression, poverty, death and destruction.
A world where the weak slowly die
Yet the strong get richer as they march on by.

We must resolve to look to our future
And promise now our planet to nurture.
For if we ignore nature's increasing warnings
We'll celebrate few more new year mornings.
What matter then if resolutions are broken
Once Mother Nature's wrath is awoken?
Mankind will be into oblivion hurled,
And take along with it what's left of our world.

Cath Conroy

ANXIETY

How is it possible,
Don't say it's no use,
There has to be an answer
She cannot just be let loose?
Care in the community,
What's the meaning of that?
She hasn't looked after herself
Never lived alone in a flat.
We all know she'll be terrified
Won't put her head outside the door,
Has this been properly thought out,
It has to be thought through some more?
Look, she has always been institutionalised
Ever since she was a child,
Taking her out now,
Will simply drive her wild.
We are her closest kin,
Don't we have a say?
Oh, there must be some mistake,
Where's that letter that came today?
We all want what's best for her,
Of that there is no doubt,
But we can't help feeling,
She won't be happy to come out.

Charles Trail

SPRING FRESH

Clusters of white snowdrops delicate heads bowed
yellow and purple crocuses standing proud
a mix and match of colour signalling go
a green light for the arrival of spring
early flowering shrubs covered in swelling buds
vulnerable to lingering frost tender parts exposed
germinating seeds of oak, beech and maple
force themselves skywards in search of sun
birds large and small begin their annual search
hunting for next sites, secret and safe
emerging daffodils in suits of green and yellow
joined by the sweet cloying smell of fragrant hyacinths
squirrels and hedgehogs stir from deep slumber
rubbing sleep from their eyes, stretching rested muscles
sharp showers of sleet and hail clear the air
leaving everything smelling spring fresh

Chris Birkitt

A NEW YEAR

A new year - a new idea.
Here's what I've *resolved* to do -
Rewrite that half-penned poem
And send it off to you.
Rewind my life and pause to see
Why it needs a fresh start.
Rekindle my enthusiasm for last year's
Nearly works of art!
Renew old friendships and *review*
Letters I must write.
The list is endless, when seen in black on white.
Rethread my needle and *refurbish* that old chair.
Be *reconciled* with my neighbour -
Can't *remember* why animosity is there!
Restart that lengthy novel
Recapture what I've read.
Rethink what else I've forgotten -
The garden - what more can be said?
New leaves, new shoots, new flowers, new fruits.
In a garden, as in life, the year *re-roots*.
If by December I can *redeem* in part
Some of these things not done,
Then January 1998 sees time *reclaimed,*
I'm *reformed, replete,* the race *re-run.*

Susan Holmquist

A RECITATION

It is a must, on New Year's Eve
The list is much the same;
I must do this,
I won't do that,
The 'resolution game'.

The sheet is clean,
No thumbprints show,
No blemishes are there,
The pristine page
All neatly writ, repeated every year.

The game's afoot
The Bard declared;
So, I shall start the morrow,
To act the scenes
With a new script.
Then life serene will follow.

But woe is me;
the 'this is hard'
and, 'that is what I do'.
On New Year's Day
I break the lot.
I always do. Do you?

Sheila Blackler

HOGMANAY

H ands clasp - old hearts ache - happiness
O vershadowed momentarily, as clocks chime to
G reet a new year. Generations of
M emories and tears flood into yet
A nother year. Once again the pain eases.
N ew Year's Day - when
A uld acquaintance are remembered and
Y oung hearts stride into the future

Eadie Logan

SAD AND JOY

Starting my life on my own,
Don't know what to do,
You have left me to cope alone,
To see our dilemma through.

Did not think that this would be,
What would happen in my life,
I had dreams for both of us,
One was to be your wife.

This has happened well you see,
I will manage on my own,
Friends and family help me out,
Even though you have flown.

Now it's over yes I am glad,
Full joy I have at last,
A baby boy lays in my arms,
I don't think now of the past.

Jackie Farrell

SPIRITS OF CHANGE

My knights be dead; the angel bled,
Their maidens lost; the heavens fled.
And all the empire cried in woe
Whilst crowns were strewn from dignity.
The high winds flew a mighty blaze;
The children hid in parent's grave -
The blue moon shone - that nightly scene
Assures the promise of deadly seas.

No creature planned a venture,
No being whispered sound -
Yet there was one who knew too long
What was foretold and should become.
- And magic weaved her spirit's play
To heighten hopes of earth's delay.
- Would she return the spin of time?
Or set delusions of death divine?

'Foretold my queen of being dwelt -
Deceit that tore this planet's felt.
Return my world of beauty's web -
Restore the spirits of the dead.'
She spoke with love's authority,
Invoking souls of deity.
'Stand up and show they face of fiend -
The work of time shall be redeemed.'

A dragon face beheld the sky,
Yet she the strong had sensed the lie -
The creature torment: goddess proud;
He be no conflict for the heavenly bound.
'All powers that be - their faith in me;
Behold! The mirror - your parody.'

Leah Singleton

GOD BALANCE EVERYTHING

God works slowly but surely in
His divine love for us
for He does not like the balance
of His works to be upset.

There below, all forces, He will put
all things right.
They are far greater than the human might,
He always gives you the sense of His peace
for the wonders He does will never cease.

For He blows a sweet fragrance of air
to fill lands with His many blessings,
there's nothing in His great wisdom He
does not understand.
He'll touch it gently with His gentle hand.

For He is always waiting, to take us
all from our realms of despair, He's there.

Although God may be silent, He listens
for His love for us is like a gem
it sparkles and it's very rare.

For He gives us strength, courage, all we
have got to do is ask.
God does not give us burdens that
He cannot help us through.
He puts the balance right no matter
what you may think or do.

Then you get a clear vision
God is our guiding light
any time of day
yes He'll put the balance
right for you, especially when you pray.

Lucille Hope

FREEDOM

(Dedicated to the people of Tibet and East Timor)

Lord as a new year is dawning
Help us to reflect on our freedom
To worship and praise you, for such
A beautiful world, full of creatures
Great and small

Help us Lord to remember those who
Are imprisoned for the faith and are
Suffering oppression, Lord Your Son
Came into the world to be the light
Of hope, may this message bring comfort
To those denied their freedom,

Through the One who died to grant us
Freedom from death and sin, our Saviour
Jesus Christ.

Henry Alexander

RING ANY BELLS LADIES?

That's it! This time is definitely the
last,
I entertain at Christmas, and they stay
till next day's breakfast.
As they all get older, they become more
difficult to please,
By the time they leave, I'm nearly down
on my knees.
'I don't like this, he doesn't eat that'
'Oh! We can't have those - they make you
fat.'
I think - take it or leave it, I couldn't
really care less,
Roll on tomorrow, when I can clear up the
mess.
New Year's resolutions, I don't usually
make,
But this year I am - for sanity's sake!
No more of this hassle - with my hair
turning grey,
Next Christmas I've decided, I'm going
away!

Jennyen

A NEW YEAR THOUGHT

Money brings us happiness
you've often heard it said
it gets us all the things we want
it buys our daily bread.

We fight and live and die for it
we even rob and kill
we lie and cheat and crave for it
then we leave it in a will,

Our dreams are all for money
we never have enough
we do the pools with fingers crossed
we idolise the stuff.

Suppose they took it all away
and no-one had a bean
what would we have to worship
and what would be our dream.

How would we occupy our minds
what would we find to do
no need to make a living
or save for something new.

So seeing that it's here to stay
wouldn't it be nice
to do something for someone
and not to ask a price?

Sylvia Iveson

HOPE A REALITY

As we end a year of glum and gloom.
Let's hope the coming year will improve soon.
More thought given to the elderly, infirm and ill.
'Twould be a good start if those at risk have their needs fulfilled.

We owe it to those who toiled in their day
For a living and sometimes meagre pay.
But the employers in that day knew within their heart.
That here was a generation who played their part.

So in the new year the objective should be tender loving care.
The NHS should be seen to be fair.
The Patients Charter could be referred to before decisions
are made.
Quality of life a priority, for those folk requiring aid.

The new year can be a renewal time.
Good for the body and good for the soul.
Physical and spiritual needs catered for, yours and mine.
If we come to the Saviour He'll fulfil that role.

Resolutions will be made, but few will last.
As the trials we face, our resolutions will soon pass.
If we come to Jesus we can turn over a new leaf.
He will forgive us and His love in our heart will keep.

God will save us if only we pray.
The Holy Spirit will guide us by night and day.
Thank God too for His blessings too.
He'll walk with you and guard you for He is a friend so true.

This coming year can be one of hope.
As our love is extended to others we will cope.
Let envy and hatred be a thing of the past.
The love of God built in our hearts to last.

Elizabeth Swaile

GRIM RESOLUTION

This last year has changed my life from the green
Of innocence to the brown of decay.
The leaves of my love, with a golden sheen,
Have fallen and died at the death of day.
For twelve months I've failed and fallen apart
And withered and weakened in winter gales.
For twelve months I've bled from wounds to the heart
And sunk into hell on fate's golden scales.
From the bare, broken branches of my life
Can spring's new leaves ever burst forth again?
Can some new hope shine forth to end my strife
And dethrone sorrow from its twelve month reign?
I've a resolution to end my pain;
From New Year's Day I'll never love again.

Chris Scriven

THE DARK SIDE OF LOVE

Unbelief, yet knowing,
Flaring anger built of bitterness and resentment
And troubled memories
Revisited -
      Re-awakened.
Such pain and hurt are not possible
These depths of abject misery.
Fear of the future as well as the past.
And in the now?
      Rejected -
            Unwanted -
                  Unlovely.
Unbearable, yet I bore it unknowingly,
Unendurable, yet I bore it unwittingly.
Distorted mind
Harrowed and tormented
      Silent screaming soul.
Hold my vulnerability close
What are these tears that are running down my face?
They are for me -
      Such loss.

Marjorie Haddon

NEW BEGINNINGS

Do you bite your nails,
Do you smoke cigarettes?
Do you have a messy bedroom,
Or not clean out your pets?

Well here's an opportunity
To do all these things,
With all the resolutions
The new year brings.

Time to turn over a new leaf,
A chance to look back,
To review all your wrongs and mistakes
                              in the past.

To think of the good and kind deeds
                        that you've done,
To look to the future,
The new life you've begun.

Rachel Hobbs

THRESHOLD

(Isaiah 43 v 2)

Thank you Lord
for the year that is past:
for all the good,
for bringing good
out of not-so-good:
for shining Your light.

Thank you Lord
for the people's lives
you have used to touch mine
with Your life:
for shining Your light

Father, as I stand
on the brink
of the river of life,
that flows into the coming year,
take my hand
and lead me
in the current of your love.
Amen.

Andrea M Koenders-Donnan

BACK IN '97

Not so much a New Year resolution,
more of a New Year wish.
An appeal, I feel I have to make,
for love, for harmony, concord and peace.

For an *end* to hostility, to war and terrorism;
For people to be happy, to leave other people alone.
For children to be safe, happy at play and well fed;
For parents to feel easy, at work, at play, at home.

For prices (ha ha!) to come down and the Tories to say bye-bye;
(please)
For a government who puts the people's needs at heart.
For death, doom and discord to vanish from the world;
For once happy people to stay in love, together, not apart.

For pathetic 'singers' without talent to be abducted by aliens;
For children to have the smiles put back on their faces.
For crime to end, sack the judges and the law to work properly;
For the homeless to be given homes and taken from dank, cold places.

For pollution to recede to save this pitiful world of ours,
to that end everyone working together, as one;
For illness to be eradicated, a new view to good health must come;
For fear of death and injury be gone along with the law of the gun.

For animals to live happily, in the wild, that is their right;
For cruelty to stop in whatever category.
For peace of mind for all in life, wherever they may be;
For my car to start in the morning without, having a flat battery!

Apart from these and more too many to mention,
I should like to see, what I class as, the next best thing to
heaven,
apart, of course, from peace, good luck and happiness for my loving
family,
I should love to see, if he's alive, Elvis to come back, in '97 . . .

Ron Matthews Jr

NEW LEAVES

As the new year nears again
I think of what I said before,
The resolutions that I made
On the last New Year's Eve,
I then resolved to love my wife
More than the year before,
And I resolved to spend more time
With our precious children,
But those were the easy ones
With those I was successful,
But in those self-regarding acts
My resolve was not so strong,
I agreed with things I knew unjust,
I patronised for my gain
And said things I knew were lies,
So as I sit on this new eve
My resolutions are more modest,
I resolve to face myself,
To truly learn what I really am
Which is not an easy thing to do,
For I am a politician.

Richard Reeve

NEW BEGINNINGS

Ascend hills above wind-break poplars
To see green fields shimmering and broody
Slope down from hedges to the shore.
Watch full-blown flowers shed their petals
Leaving deep scents drifting on the breeze.
Unseen birds are chirping stridently
Secretive in trees below the long hill's summit.
Far below a finger of sea basks in sensuous repose
Until clean, white sand welcomes the booming breakers.
Eyes weary with wonder, look upwards to the sky
In agitation of colour from the near-diminished sun.
Seagulls spin and plummet to the cliffs below
Remote from nature's warmth of turf and spray.
Lie on your back on these high, warm hills
Leave passing friends to chatter like the birds;
Old loves to fade as flowers wilt and die.
Face the breakers when they reach the shore
And make a new beginning with the freedom of a gull.

Nancy Reeves

THE GHOST

Sunlight steals through the dusty rooms
Full of books and lighted gloom
Windows small such thin paned glass
A breath of air to paint the past

Floorboards bare
The old fireplace
'Twas where I used to play
My father had a smiley face
That one day went away

Mother had her old chair
Where she would sit and sew
And look at me once in a while
With thoughts I did not know

And here the clock ticked on the wall
Sometimes friend, sometimes foe
The finger of time pointing its way
Sometimes night, sometimes day
And how those years have passed away.

Rachel Knighton

I CAN BUT ASK FORGIVE

I can but ask, forgive,
bid sorrow slip away;
Ask thee let me live,
In peace of mind today.
I can but say, my thoughts didst move,
In circles distant from their course;
My yesterday was twice removed,
From kindliness at thy fair source.
So sweep away all bitterness,
Allow me step toward thy heart;
Compassion, source of greatest bliss,
Return from where it once did start.
My heart toward thee fills anew,
My soul, twixt thine, its purpose true.

David Beecroft

LOOKING FORWARD

A new year begins but don't be down
Drive away that wintry frown
Days that shortened now get longer
Thoughts of spring are growing stronger

It's fresh, it's cold, the air is clean
There's lots to enjoy in the outside scene
Find your coat and scarf and go out walking
Take a friend and do some talking

Life is too precious to waste a day
So do things, dream things, laugh and play
Bring on the crocus and daffodil flower
The sun is giving the earth its power

The birds are excited in their quest
To find a mate and build a nest
In pots, old kettles, hedges, boxes, shed and loft
Are meshes of twig and pieces soft

Worms and grubs in earth are stirring
Wings of millions of insects whirring
Colours are bright in everything
All is life and this is spring

Now lingering mists come with the dawning
Warm sun bathes us all from morning
On till late then orange sinking
Time of plenty, eating, drinking

Then rusty, yellow, brown and red
As Dame Autumn leaves her bed
Coloured carpets lay on forest floors
Time to paint and varnish doors!
Make the soup and wine and beer
Be thankful for another year!

Steve McIlroy

IF I COULD - I WOULD

My New Year resolutions I will try to keep,
Unlike others that only lasted for a week,
I'll stop smoking and drinking wine,
Goodbye to unhealthy nights on the town,

No more pizzas, burgers or Chinese,
I'll slip into my new life with great ease,
Imagine all the money I could save,
And I might even lose that extra bit of weight,

I'll have cosy nights watching TV,
I can read books and play my CD's,
While my friends will be going out to clubs,
Not to mention the numerous pubs,

They'll probably meet lots of cool guys,
While I'm watching 'Stars in Their Eyes',
Wines and beers no doubt will be flowing,
I'll be at home living healthy and boring,

My resolutions I may have to rethink,
I can't do it - I miss a cigarette and a drink,
Honestly I've tried at least for a day and a half,
I just miss being social and having some laughs,

So, I've reached a conclusion you may understand,
What's a life without junk food, beer and men,
I'm no good at staying home all on my own,
Goodbye resolutions - where's the phone?

Tracey Thomson

Nature's Way

Of the writing of books there is no end.
As in creative art and lovely music we ever depend.
Inspiring sounds of song - life's joy these blessings bring.
Akin to pretty poetry the bluebird sings merrily on wing.
Our dear feathered friends build their nests in sunny spring.
Perfected in detail each precious leaf on tree and flower.
Sweet scented stock and yellow daffodil grow tall in April's shower.
While red and gold butterfly glow with prideful power.
In field the newly born lamb tends to frolic in summer's air.
Busy bees making honey their wisdom supremely rare.
Red robin returns as our winter's season draws nigh.
Unique shapes of white snowflake fall softly 'neath a misty sky.
Autumn's tree sheds its worn leaves - how soon 'tis so bare.
Until again they'll grow strong with God's tender love and care.
Such wonders of nature surround us year by year.
Regardless of passing time through the ageless process of prayer.

Eleanor Haydon Sanderson

IMAGINATION

What if I could write from my imagination,
See myself in a strange situation.
Wouldn't that be fun for my mind.
Maybe get drawn into some kind of crime.

I could even rob a bank,
Be a soldier who drives a tank
Or leads an army into war.
Be a football player who never fails to score.

End up in the wild west,
A gunslinger who, always draws the best.
A pop singer who's the biggest in the world
Always chased by screaming girls.

Why not a leading man in a movie,
Being cool and really groovy.
Save a maiden from an ivory tower.
Being strong with lots of power.

Or a comedian who is very funny.
Holy man searching for the land of milk and honey.
An astronaut out in space,
A detective working on a case.

Yet instead all I can do is to recall,
And that's not too much fun at all.

R C Price

FALLING INTO TOMORROW

Falling into tomorrow,
Letting time show the value of today,
Making future decisions,
That may keep our minds at bay,
So much to show how the value of our living,
Is the essence of this vast puzzle.

Where time reaches to the ultimate,
Perhaps travelling so many miles away,
Falling into tomorrow, letting troubled images
seem to be more tame.

Showing that life in the first place,
Cannot be previewed,
As just a game,
Of course there is another factor,
That we have overlooked,
That is how we sample,
The many wonders that count for everything,
On our globe itself that entails.

Colin Hush

STIRRINGS

When loosened from evil's bonds
The spirit stirs.
The birds that were silent
Come out and sing.
The flowers and green shoots
Choked with briars and weeds
Come out and bloom.
The waters, that were stagnant and turbid,
Flow free in limpid brooks and clear pools,
Mirrors to the sky, the lush foliage, the flowers.
A young girl blows a surging flute tenderly.

Angela Cutrale Matheson

A LASS FRAE INVERARAY

I went a trip in early May tae Inveraray toon
The sun was oot and so was I ma broo was turnin' broon
And then I spied a braw wee lass walkin' by the pier
So I daunered doon there by myself and then began tae spier

She was Mary frae Inveraray and she was like a fairy
The way she walks and the way she talks
Just had me in her spell
But time went by and I had to go, she had tae go as well
So I said goodbye tae Mary frae Inveraray

When I got back tae Glesca toon, Mary was in my mind
I vowed that I'd return one day in hoping I would find
The braw wee lass I met that day walkin' by the pier
This time it would be different I widnae need tae spier

She was Mary frae Inveraray she works doon in the dairy
The way she walks and the way she talks
Still has me in her spell
If she says 'yes' when I propose tae a' the folk I'll tell
That I've won the brawest lass in Inveraray

S T Jennings

AWAITING NEW YEAR

Three hundred and sixty four days in a year go by,
Yet no-one takes heed until the last ten seconds are nigh.

In those last few moments we stand breathless and await,
Waiting for eternity, forgetting anger and hate.

As the last second ticks by we scream, sing, jump and cheer,
For now the old year is history and the new one here.

Kevin Stevens

NO RESOLUTION

As the old year ends,
And the new one begins
We all resolve,
To give up our sins.

It may be no smoking,
Or cut down on drink.
How many will win?
Not many I think.

So I have decided,
This year to refrain
From making a promise,
To save all the pain.

I'll not be a loser,
I'll be a kind friend,
Do lots of good deeds,
My bad ways, I will mend.

But listen to me!
I'm at it again.
It's always the way,
It's always the same.

Kathleen Wakefield

RECALLING LOVE

The first time that our eyes met 'across that crowded room'
What you felt was romance, what I felt was doom.
The thing that's so amazing is not that it's now finished
but that the flame burned brightly and never was diminished.
You saw a safe harbour - just where you'd want to be
I always wanted to 'up anchor' and forever put to sea

We each approached life from completely different directions
different memories, different cultures and different affections
It's not just that the packaging of ourselves is simply a different colour
your wrapping a shade of pastel whilst mine is a vibrant fuller
search for something to build a really exciting life
when what you wanted was a second mate, a housekeeper, a wife

Though there is no question of the depth of my love for you
there never was a time when there was anything I could do
to alter the course of my particular storm-tossed little ship
to the moment of its wrecking from its time on the launching slip
Until the time for me to go 'into that bright tomorrow'
our parting, which was inevitable, will be remembered with great
sorrow

'Whom God hath joined together let no man put asunder'
No man did, it was all my fault and so I'll always wonder
why all the bitterness developed when we could have parted as good
friends
It can't have been all the lawyer's fault, our own behaviour offends
my sense of justice - the things we said to each other in anger
cannot be forgotten (someday forgiven?) forever there'll be the danger

that our final words could expunge memories of our years together
if your regret for that is as deep as mine I wonder whether
we could meet (I'd say I'm sorry) not to start again
but just to touch, one last time, to ease a bit the pain
of a loss that seems to grow deeper as the years go past
We both were hurt. I'm truly sorry. I will be to the last.

Florence B Broomfield

I MEAN IT THIS YEAR ...

Every December it's always the same,
We sit down and play 'the resolutions game'.
We sit in our chairs in front of the fire,
The mountain of paper growing higher and higher.

Our lists always start 'I mean it this year'
I will give up cigarettes, whisky or even the beer.
We take a deep breath when we think of the waste,
But we did write the list with no thought, just haste.

The New Year is the time to start
To play the game with all your heart.
But when New Year comes upon us again,
You think, 'Oh no! I've lost my list again.'

Gaynor Cowell

NEW BEGINNINGS

One day a door just opened and
A new world I could see.
I didn't know what a difference
This was going to mean to me.

To see things in a different light
To be positive and sure
To know that what I feel is right
Thank heavens for that door.

I don't wish that door to close now
I've seen things that I like
I've waited such a long time
And I know that this is right.

Janet Williams

MY SISTER SARAH FROM JOSHUA LEE

Eight months of waiting
    With my sister Sarah
Waiting to enter the world
How could we know then
Only one of us
    Was going to survive the birth

We were so close to each other
Oh so closely entwined
Nothing would ever part us
As we dreamed in our mother's womb

But cruel fate intercepted
In the shape of a hospital nurse
In too much of a hurry to birth us
I was born brain damaged and worse

Fit after fit I encountered
Until at last my poor body was still
And the decision to free me was taken
At mummy and daddy's will

I'll never play with you on earth
But I see you come to my grave
I know you feel me near you
By the light upon your face

And now it's Christmas time again
And a toy to me you bring
I hear 'Away in a Manger'
As once more to me you sing.

So I'll just stay here with grandad
Till you pass through heaven's door
Then we will be together once again
    'Twins' forever more.

Joy Nethercot

THE FORTHCOMING

They had fallen,
And lay upon the ground,
Red, yellow and brown,
Their host stood naked now
Like great giants
Rooted to the spot,
And the end was the beginning
Of the new.
The long shadows had returned
Once again,
To haunt the beautifully sad,
The wind now blew its
Unpleasant coldness
With a whispering chill
As the warmth of summer
Echoed far far away,
To the forthcoming of
Winter days.

Kevin Michael Jones

Usutu

Full flotilla, full speed steaming,
An enemy to find.
Entering now home waters,
'Piping peace' left far behind.

From the first ferocious winter
'Lifebelts must be worn!'
Your body belongs to the Admiralty,
Your soul may be your own.

Have a bath, change your shift,
As the War Orders said.
It seems for these divisions,
You must be clean: tho' dead.

Altmark, Narvik, Bismark.
Iceland's perishing blow.
Bombardments and landings,
Burning cargoes' mocking glow.

Battle ensigns laid flat aft,
Gulf of Sirte fights.
Pedestal, Halberd, convoys.
The cheering Malta Heights.

Ships' companies, shaped, from rival pranks.
Regattas in the sun,
Sports, and upper deck uckers,
Trophies to be won.
Fulfilled their promise, blanching trials,
Dangers shipmates share,
Refining life and character
Criticise them, if you dare.

Ray Dite

THE POPPY

A drift of red among the golden corn,
Poppies, brilliant in the summer morn,
Each graceful flower, perfect in every way,
Beauty, captured and displayed for one short day.
Its petals falling in the evening air,
Replaced tomorrow with a bloom as fair.

Likewise in Flanders, where our young men stood,
The flower of youth, the proud, the brave, the good.
To be wiped out with gas, with shells, with fire.
Felled and buried in the noisome mire.
Next day, more soldiers came to take their place.
More, en' thousands more, the gruesome slaughter face.

Was it by design, or some uncanny chance,
The poppy is the emblem of remembrance?
In the killing fields of Flanders,
Where the youth of Britain lie.
Poppies stretch like a sea of blood,
Bloom for a day, then die.

Daphne White

THE RANKS OF DEATH

We would have savoured the dawning day,
Cherished our children, watched them at play,
Travelled life's cycle of pleasure and pain,
Smiled with the sun, cried with the rain,
Smelt the flowers, breathed the air . . .
. . . Lived to the full each passing year.

We didn't grow old, we warrior men;
Not for us, three-score-and-ten.
A sniper's bullet, a bomb, a shell,
Some ghastly weapon devised in Hell
Plucked us, savagely, from the fight -
- So short a day . . . so long a night.

One day, the world will heed God's law
And turn its back on endless war,
Banishing thoughts of 'friend-or-foe.'
Then, peace shall reign. We dead shall know
That, when mankind vows: 'Never again!'
Our sacrifice was not in vain.

Alan Titley

CHRISTMAS WISH

This is my Christmas wish:
To gather round some friendly hearth
Our scattered friends from all about the world.
From the five continents and seven seas, by every path
From tents, or desert aerodrome from wards
In far off hospitals, from squadron, camps and ships.

We have come far together, we have seen
Promise re-fashioned out of failure.
Rescue and courage beating down despair
Into a shining triumph;
So let each recall
Now, in the burning light of hope,
The days we struggled grimly in the dark.

Now Christmas bells can ring again in England
Sound without dread calling across the sea.
Ringing for those who have not lived to hear them;
While we who hear them, hear quietly
Through our shared past.
Now we can see our future in the shared fire.
The New Year holds for us a desperate challenge -
Let this be our resolve.
We shall not tire.

C A Beard

GREATER LOVE HATH NO MAN

Among the fields of Flanders
And the stillness of the Somme,
Are graves both known and unknown
Of those whose deeds were done

In the name of Hope and Freedom,
Obedient to the last
To the orders of their leaders,
To those who saw the past

As the gateway to the future,
No matter what the cost;
But graves bear silent witness
To those who fought and lost . . .

Their lives were given in sacrifice
So the rest of us might live;
Two minutes, and the price of a poppy,
Is all we're asked to give.

We'll recall, as we stand in silence,
Those who died in the Hell of The Somme;
And remember, lest we forget, the brave
Who, like Christ, fought Hell, and won . . .

J Margaret Service

OUR OMEGA

Far from home, in war-torn France,
Escape seemed blocked, without a chance of breaking free,
Till suddenly Fate smiled on me . . .
I fled the dreaded fear of Dachau's Camp
And boarded ship - a coaling - 'tramp,'
Whose 'cargo' was the same as me: folks who had to try and flee
The tread-mill race of 'Hunter's Chase,'
From the terror-squads of Nazi Hoards,
Who requested forced and cruel 'rewards' . . .

The Past was past! Our future now was ocean-bound - our mighty
convoy sailed!
Trans-shipped, was I, to 'Troop-Dunera' - because 'Ashcrest's engines
failed -
Ever west towards the Sun, the Captains stood by ready gun
To steer a game of deadly chess -
A zig-zag course, to counter loss, and make the hazards less
From 'Subs' beneath the sea -
Because they were there, those submarines; and their periscopes could
see . . .

With spying Argo eyes, torpedoes struck the tankers till volcanoes lit
the
skies -
And nought was left but death - profane, grotesque - and sullen oil-slick
lies . . .
The war-ships brought what they could find - bodies of lives lost -
We took them from their caring hands - we prayed for them without the
bands -
For they had paid the Cost.

The horrors of these Hydra-frays will live with me for all my days . . .

Home at last, with anchor cast, my Father came to me -
But as a stranger, from the past, was all that I could see -
But then the truth soon dawned on me! It was a camouflage I saw!
He wore a uniform! A uniform of war!
But on his shoulder was a flash -
In red-and-white it glared at me - hostile as unwanted trash -
Then, as in a nightmare guessing-game, I read one single headline name:
Okinawa . . . So, it was, for him, another War - of which he had no earthly blame.

Dorothea R Payn Le Sueur

BATU LINTANG

It was on a hill at Batu Lintang my story comes to life,
Of guns, of gunners, of infantiers that caused a lot of strife.

At night a gun and mortar too was hard to fire loud.
The night was dark, the air was damp, the sky was full of cloud.

'Take post!' The cry that carried far. Take post the gunners did.
They ran so fast they left their beers, the cans with holes in lid.

The TARA by the director stand with pencil torch and board in hand,
called out the bearing for the line to the gunners who were there on
time.

The number one duly reported 'Centre of Arc recorded.'
On night RO he had laid his gun and its from here my story comes.

The order came for guns to fire, '26 rounds you must not tire,'
but after six there came a shout. 'Hey! Hey! The light's gone out.'
The layer shouted 'Hey it's gone some one turn the light back on.'

The number one on prism lay and for rest of shoot that's
where he stayed.

The Troop Commander and Australian chap could not stand by and
hear all that. So out he went and to the place found the Company
Commander with red face.

'I say, I say, what have you done? Surely this not for fun?'
'No, no, I had a fright because of brightness of the light'
'At first I thought there was a spy because of torch on hut up high'
'To late' my Mortar Sergeant said 'no that's the gunners night RO.'

The story ends or so it's said when all the gunners were in bed
Of beer, of rum, of curry too. But that my friends is not for you.

T W Stimson

RICHARD'S WAR

R ichard was a soldier in the RGJ's
I t was his dream all of his school days.
- he
C herished the years spent as a Rifleman, serving our Queen
H e planned to spend all his life around the army scene.
A tour of Northern Ireland was almost at an end.
R ichard was on duty patrolling with his friend.
D arkness came and a riot broke out very quick
S adly Richard's career was ended when hit by a brick.

W e now live with epilepsy by the calming sea
A rmy life for Richard was really not to be.
R ichard was a soldier serving in *Peace* time
- I'm a lucky wife to have him whole and mine!

Elaine Duggan

SPIT AND POLISH

On parade the cry rings out
What the heck's it all about?
Hair off collar, cap badge clean
Battledress pressed and boots that gleam
At the double or there's trouble
What a blessing we were young
And arthritic joints were still to come!

Kathleen Jarrold

THE PALM TREE

Palm trees rustled overhead, cicadas strummed their wings,
And bullfrogs, strident, sang their songs of secret swampy things.
The moonlit sands were soft, like surf, lapping round one's feet,
And it was here that fate decreed this girl and I should meet.

When later we became engaged our good friends rallied round,
And organised a party with whatever could be found.
We made a modest gathering, just a special few,
A khaki-clad conglomerate of colleagues old and new.

Eventually, back home, I wed this girl of many charms,
And often we recalled those days of friendly waving palms.
Years later when we came across a tiny potted palm
We bought it and we thought it made a living lucky charm.

As time went on our tree grew tall, reflecting our contentment,
Then when my dear wife passed away it seemed to feel resentment.
Its leaves turned brown, it hung its head, it wilted without warning,
As if it recognised and shared the sorrow and the mourning.

In time it lifted up its head, regaining its full height,
And then a crown of buds appeared, tipped with tufts of white.
Soon there was a riot of bloom - exotic, bright with cheer -
In glorious celebration of the one I held so dear.

F Jensen

EVACUATION 1939

Let the new Doomsday be written,
Not the beauclerk's tale after Senlac;
Sullen Saxon defiance, the Conqueror's orderly pillage,
Enserfment, and the totting of corn mills and purlieus,
The halt, laborious screed of vill and vert and tillage.

Write the new chronicle;
The children of Saxon and Norman
Orderly leaving the cities in face of a bloodier danger;
Fosterage, and the listing of billets and houses and beds;
The human tally of kindness, and a welcome hearth for the stranger -
      These let a new clerk write.

Maisie Herring

THE AGONY RETURNS

We were not at war we were swapping bullets,
participating 'cause we were told to do it
and while we waited, we bared our souls
in loving letters that we sent home.

And whilst we played with guns and knives
we would speculate about our lives.
Whilst we waited, we often kissed
the photographs of the ones we missed.

Our hollowed eyes had watched friends die,
we prayed that *peace* would come.
Our women wept as the children slept,
Now - the Agony returns,
to the blooded nights and War torn sights
that have scarred man's Heart and Soul,
As the poppies fall from heaven
many memories unfold.

Of Friends who died for Freedom
who have died for you, for me,
so that future generations
could bring aggression to its knees.

So east and west, could lay to rest
their threats, Today, Forever.
To Think aloud, what's life about
before, they pull the Trigger.

Alan Glendinning

PRIVATE ROSS

Front line obnoxious
Month after month,
Home life oblivious
Devoid of its worth.
An enemy so avid
Trenches of mud
Blood and corpses rigid
Mind terror flood.
Mustard gas explodes
Masks on in time
Technology did exclude
The safety zone.
Where was sentiment
Where was the glory
Imagination figment
An unimaginable story.
Medals on ribbon
Kept in a box
Recollections and sobbing
A gentleman; broke:

George Livingston Shand

FUNGI

A shadow on the step is all I see
        amidst the desolation.

A little girl sat there
her elbows resting on her knees
hands gently cradling her chin
watching pensively the city
walking to a summer day.

A flash of light
only her shadow left
blotting for ever humanity's soul
an indelible reproach
Hiroshima.

B J Bramwell

REMEMBRANCE

Fifty years on, but where have they gone?
As memories come to us now that still linger on.
We give thanks for all those years of peace,
And pray that in time, all wars shall cease.
For those who gave their lives to save us then,
May we never ever forget our debt to them.
And now, today, may each of us in our own way,
Look to the future with Faith and Hope and say:
Now and forever we shall always remember them.

And then, as with the passing of the years,
We try to hide the sorrow and the tears,
And with our faces changing and growing lined,
We will always try to keep in mind,
Those who did not return, like me and you -
Or lived to see their dreams come true.
The pains that we suffer may be the signs of age,
But having now lived our span on this world's stage,
If God shall give us that bit of extra time to play,
Let us give him now our thanks for each and every day.

Albert W Bennett

TWO WISE MEN

December 1939 and a letter came through the door
With trembling hands I opened it and read the words *war*
My calling-up papers had arrived, in the Army I must go
'You will report to Waterloo Station and prepare to fight the foe'
We arrived at Woolwich Station and were marched to the barracks there
And immediately upon arrival paraded on the barrack square
The Sergeant seemed an uncouth lout and bawled and spat out his
                                                                orders
'What do you want to call yourselves,' he yelled, 'Blankety Blank
                                                                soldiers?'
I can still hear his voice ringing in my ears
And some of us were reduced to tears
Was it going to be like this every day?
Was he always going to shout that way?
Perhaps it was the treatment we had half expected
Notwithstanding the fact that we felt dejected
Life would be hard he told us then
Just listen and learn and react like men
Take heed of my warning and think with your head
Then you'll come back safely and not finish up dead
We thought him a bully but an old soldier was he
As wise and as wise as a man can be
For during my Service in foreign lands
Over mountainous country and desert sands
I remembered that Sergeant and the words he had said
For I'm still alive and this can be read.
Thank you Sergeant.

Ronald J Buzzle

THE BREATHLESS BLUE

I have tasted the very breath of God
  In the vast unfathomed skies,
Alone in the sunlit heights I've trod
  Cut off from all earthly ties.

Where the white clouds race on the laughing wind,
  Pursued by a golden sun,
I've wheeled and turned in my craft, to find
  Her eager to enter the fun!

Oh, the joy of a loop and the thrill of the dive!
  With an engine's crescendo roar;
The bracing wires tremble, the wings are alive
  And respond as we dip and we soar.

But earth's far call at last must subdue
  This spirit of freedom and play,
Lest I drink too much in the breathless blue
  And, drunken, am tempted to stay.

Peter B Wills

INFORMATION

We hope you have enjoyed reading this book - and that you will continue to enjoy it in the coming years.

If you like reading and writing poetry drop us a line, or give us a call, and we'll send you a free information pack.

Write to :-

Anchor Books Information
1-2 Wainman Road
Woodston
Peterborough
PE2 7BU